Nature Walks in

DORSET

• SOUTH AND WEST •

Nature Walks in

DORSET

• SOUTH AND WEST •

Tim Goodwin

DORSET BOOKS

First published in Great Britain in 1997

British Library Cataloguing-in-Publication Date
A CIP record for this title is available from the British Library

ISBN 1 871164 32 X

DORSET BOOKS
Official publisher to Dorset County Council
Halsgrove House
Lower Moor Way
Tiverton EX16 6SS
Tel: 01884 243242
Fax: 01884 243325

Printed and bound in Great Britain by The Devonshire Press, Torquay

CONTENTS

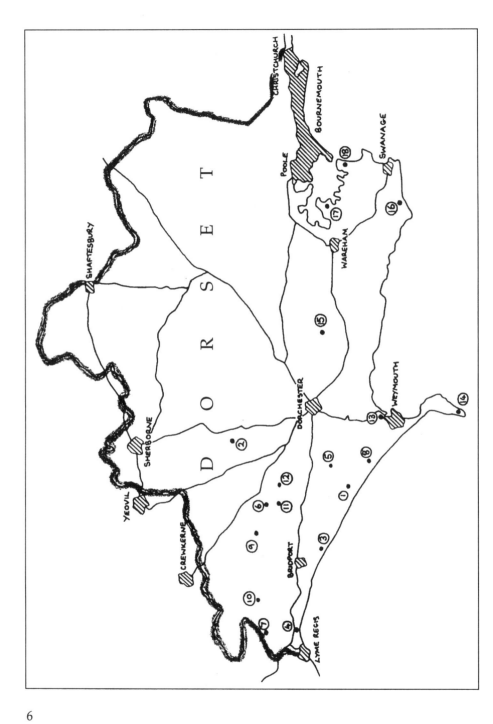

INTRODUCTION

South and West Dorset are among the most attractive parts of England and the natural history of the area is rich and varied. Because of the mild winters, many southern species of plant, insect and bird are on, or close to, their northern limits, while the almost unique Dorset heaths are home to flora and fauna that can be seen nowhere else in Britain. South and West Dorset are unsurpassed throughout Britain for reptiles, butterflies and dragonflies, as well as being possibly the best region of the south coast for birds, with Portland attracting an astonishing number of rarities every year.

As Dorset is also famously picturesque, these walks, most of which represent roughly half a day's not-too-strenuous walking, offer superb opportunities for walkers who like to see beautiful countryside, while savouring natural history. They have been designed to cover a wide variety of habitats and scenery, spaced fairly evenly through the region. The walks have been worked out with drivers in mind, and are all circular.

The descriptions do not, of course, list more than a tiny proportion of what may be seen, but I have tried to strike a balance between things that walkers will certainly see if they go at the right time of year; things they may see; and a few genuine rarities that have been seen in the area. There are also brief notes about nearby pubs and places for refreshment, and about other sights that can be seen on the walks.

Sketch maps are provided, but walkers are recommended to purchase relevant maps in the OS Pathfinder series for more detailed information.

1

ABBOTSBURY

HOW TO GET THERE

Just north of the village of Abbotsbury on the B3157 take the turning marked to the Sub-Tropical Gardens. Drive to the seashore, where there is a car park on the left (small charge in summer).

LENGTH AND SEASON

10 miles. All year.

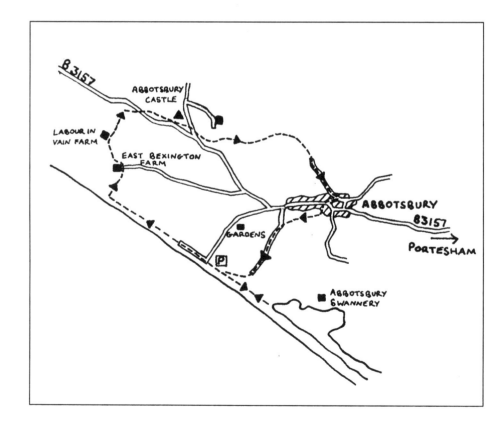

THE WALK

Walk north up the beach beside a Tamarisk hedge, which can contain bird rarities in autumn. There are Rabbits and Foxes on the hillside. Migrant butterflies such as Painted Lady, Red Admiral, and Clouded Yellow visit. The shingle has Sea Kale, a maritime form of Bittersweet, Sea Campion, Yellow Horned Poppy. Stonechats, Pipits and Finches are common. Offshore there are Gulls, Common, Sandwich and sometimes Little Terns in summer, a few Auks and Divers in winter, a few years back a young Humpback Whale visited.

After about a mile and a half, turn right up a path waymarked to the hill fort. Alexanders line the path. Pass through the farmyard, ignoring the road on the right, and follow the yellow arrows crossing the field to Labour in Vain Farm, then turning right up Tulk's Hill. There are Blackberry thickets, Sloes, Bryony, Hartstongue ferns. Look for Warblers and Flycatchers in early summer. At the top turn right (signposted Hardy Monument), cross the main road and continue to the hill fort. Skylarks are common and some species of meadow fungi. At the top, 705 feet high, are Rock Rose, patches of Heather, and magnificent views. Grasshoppers are numerous.

Cross a side road and carry on along the ridge as it swings round to the east. Stonechats call in the scrub, Kestrels hover overhead; there are tumuli on the left. Two miles beyond the hill-fort turn right by the sign-post to Abbotsbury. On a rocky, eroded outcrop there is Wild Thyme, Salad Burnet, many sorts of Lichen. Look for Common Blue butterflies, Bee Orchid and Autumn Gentian. Buzzards hunt the fields. Continue down the hill, through waymarked gates into a lane down into Abbotsbury, with Holm Oaks.

In the village turn right, right again along the main road, then left into Chapel Lane, lined with flower garden escapes. With St Catherine's chapel ahead, swing right following the sign to Chesil Bank. Green Woodpeckers hunt the fields for Ants' nests. Turn left where lanes meet. The hedgerows have Wild Rose, Honeysuckle, Campion, Ladder Ferns.

Pheasants are numerous. Follow the signpost to West Bexington. There is a stream on the right with Comfrey, Gladdon, and several species of Damselfly and Dragonfly including the Golden-Ringed Dragonfly and Broad-Bodied Libellula. Keep straight down to the beach by the Tamarisk hedge. Large Volvariella fungi grow in the autumn.

At the beach turn left through reeds which support Sedge and Reed Warblers in summer and in winter often have Cetti's Warbler and Water Rail. Wild Celery grows by the path and there are more Dragonflies. Watch out for Scarlet Tiger and Burnet moths. Continue to the tank traps for a view over the Fleet. In summer there are large flocks of Mute Swan and nesting Terns, in winter massive rafts of Duck include Shoveler, Pochard, Tufted Duck, Wigeon, Gadwall, Teal and Pintail. Kingfishers, Scaup and Long-Tailed Duck are fairly regular. Garganey occasionally visit in spring, Little Egret, Spoonbill and Osprey in autumn. Grebes are always present. The beach is the Dorset stronghold of the Sea Pea, and also has Shrubby Sea-Blite, Sea Beet and Sea Kale. The area is worth checking for Henbane, Slender Thistle, and Vipers Bugloss. Return up the beach to the car park.

REFRESHMENT
Pubs and tea shops in Abbotsbury.

2

BATCOMBE – UP CERNE

HOW TO GET THERE

Take the A352 from Dorchester towards Sherborne. Just past Minterne Magna turn left along a minor road. Two miles along turn into Batcombe Picnic Site and park there.

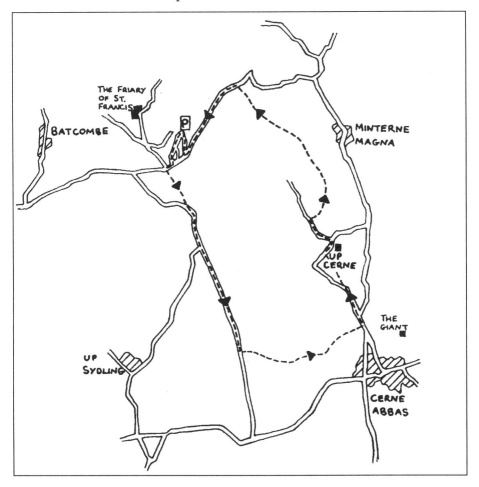

LENGTH AND SEASON

Just over 8 miles. Best, April to August.

THE WALK

Batcombe Picnic site has superb views over Somerset, Orchids in the rough grass, meadow butterflies, and several species of Warbler, including Garden Warbler, in the surrounding scrub. The woods down the hill have the unusual Duke of Burgundy Fritillary. Return to the road and turn right. By the right turn signposted The Friary take the track opposite off to the left, through a spinney thick with bluebells, with several species of tit. The path then runs by open fields with Skylarks and Yellowhammers, joining a larger farm track. Follow the main track, which is part of the Wessex Ridgeway. Deer and smaller animals, including stoats, frequently use it. Where the track swings sharp right, continue straight on, by the Ridgeway waymark. There are Skipper butterflies, Pheasants, flocks of Swifts, nesting Buzzards in the spinney on the right, and cornfield weeds – some of them quite unusual. Hobbies occasionally fly overhead, Woodlarks and Marsh Fritillaries have been seen. In winter the fields have Redwing, Fieldfare, Lapwing and Golden Plover.

Just before the radio mast turn left by a sign 'footpath only', and go through the field. At the wood turn right, then almost immediately left by a waymark into the wood. The wood is partly an old Hazel coppice, and has Bluebells, Deer, Squirrels, Speckled Woods, Blackcaps, Primroses and probably Dormice. Cut straight through the wood, cross the waymarked stile, cross the field slanting right to the gate, go through it, then follow the track through two more fields, then curve right around the foot of a hill by the fence. The ancient strip lynchets have chalk flowers, Rabbits, and a fine variety of butterflies, including Small Heath, Common Blue, Brown Argus, Chalkhill Blue, and sometimes Adonis Blue. There are good views over the Cerne Abbas giant straight ahead.

Cross the stile on the right and follow a rather overgrown path, continuing right on to a farm road. Watch for Red-Legged Partridge, not particularly common in Dorset. Turn left at the main road, then almost immediately left again along the by-road to Up Cerne. There are Whitethroats in the hedgerow, and orange Soldier Beetles in the Cow Parsley. The lake on the right has Tufted Duck, Canada Goose, Dabchick, Moorhen, Coot, and a chance of Great Crested Grebe and Kingfisher. Where the road swings left, keep straight on by a white gate and a sign 'footpath only'. Cross the field, often red with Poppies, and turn right on the road into the pretty hamlet of Up Cerne, with its ancient manor house, Green Woodpeckers in the gardens and nesting Swallows. Turn left up the by-road by a small stream with Pied and Grey Wagtails, Bullheads, Watercress, Water Speedwell. Opposite a spinney turn right by the bridle path sign, and follow it uphill into a wood with Primroses and Dog's Mercury.

At the top of the hill are two fine Turkey Oaks. The path now goes north along the right-hand edge of the wood. There are Skippers, Woodpeckers, Nuthatches, flocks of Tits, Holly trees, Grasshoppers, Brown Argus butterflies, a variety of day-flying moths including the Hummingbird Hawk-Moth, nesting Buzzards, Roe Deer, Foxes, and views over Minterne Magna. Little Owls are possible. Keep by the right-hand edge of the wood, finally emerging on the road. Turn left and follow the road through a small wood, thick with Ransoms and Bluebells in spring, and so finally turn right back into Batcombe Picnic Site.

REFRESHMENT
There are several pubs in Cerne Abbas, and the Greyhound at Sydling.

3

BURTON BRADSTOCK

HOW TO GET THERE
From Bridport take the B3157 towards Weymouth. Just past the village of Burton Bradstock the road swings sharp right. A hundred yards on is a small right turning signposted 'To the Beach'. Drive down this to the National Trust car park.

LENGTH AND SEASON
8¹/₂ miles. All year.

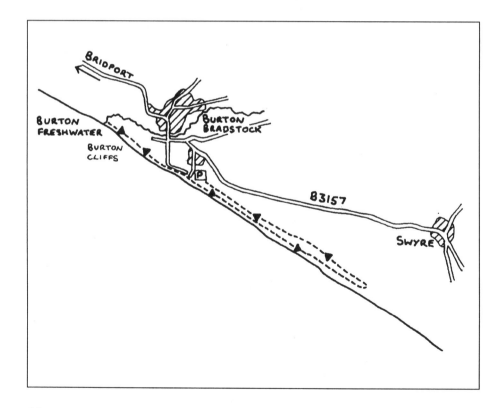

THE WALK

From the car park turn left and walk down the beach to the south. Fallen rocks under the crumbling cliffs are worth investigating for fossils – Ammonites, Belemnites, and ancient Corals. The shingle banks sometimes yield Jasper and Chalcedony. Offshore there are low-flying Cormorants, Gannets and Sandwich Terns in summer, Guillemots and Razorbills in winter. Fishing boats hunt out Mackerel, Sprats and Whiting. In hot summers Basking Sharks cruise the coast, huge numbers of Spider Crabs were seen in August 1997, and once a Bottle-Nosed Whale visited for some weeks. All along this walk there are good chances of unusual birds in spring and autumn. Recent visitors have included Hoopoe, Black-Winged Stilt, Firecrest, Wryneck, Red-Backed Shrike. The rare Lesser Cockroach can be found with patience, and there is a chance of the dramatic Jersey Tiger Moth.

After a mile the cliffs drop down to the shingle of Cogden Beach, with Sea Kale, Sea Beet, Sea Campion, Thrift and Yellow Horned Poppy. Watch out for the rare Sea Holly. Flocks of Greenfinches, Linnets and Goldfinches are common and large in autumn and winter. On the left is the reed bed of Burton Mere, home to Sedge, Reed and occasional Cetti's Warblers. Watch for a variety of damselflies and dragonflies, including the Migrant Hawker, Ruddy Darter and Golden Ringed Dragonfly. Gull flocks often gather, and in late autumn Wheatears pass by. Foxes seek out weak or unwary birds.

A mile and a half further on turn left where a footpath swings inland, then almost immediately turn left again and follow the path back north, with the reedbed on your left. The ground is thick with Silverweed, also Spotted Medick and Slender Thistle. Pipits and Skylarks are in the grass. Water Mint grows on the damp margins. The handsome Stonechat is always present. Follow the track up the cliff through the caravan site. Butterflies include Lulworth Skipper, Painted Lady, Marbled White, Red Admiral, Common Blue. The day-flying Silver Y Moth is present in late summer. Crickets and Grasshoppers are numerous in the long grass. There are scattered fungi, including Ink-Caps.

Rabbits are common but shy. Continue down to the car park, where the beach has a variable amount of sand, and some Sea Rocket, then on up the cliffs again. Kestrels hunt the fields, and there are magnificent views over Lyme Bay. A mile and a half on the cliffs descend to where the River Bride reaches the sea. There is another caravan site. Wagtails gather and late winter floods can attract Duck and more unusual birds.

Return to the car park along the beach, **unless the tide is high or rising, in which case you should return along the cliff-top path**. Rock Pipits feed on seaweed thrown up by the waves. Mermaid's Purses (egg cases of Skate and Dogfish) and Cuttlefish 'bones' are often washed up. Offshore between November and March there is generally a flock of Common Scoter, which sometimes includes Velvet Scoter and Long-Tailed Duck. Watch for Red-Throated Diver. The cliffs, heavily eroded with some short-lived caves, provide nesting sites for Fulmars, Jackdaws, Pigeons and Gulls. Ravens and Peregrines visit.

REFRESHMENT
The Hive Beach Café by the car park is open April to October. There is also the Burton Cliff Hotel and several pubs in Burton Bradstock itself.

4

CHARMOUTH – GOLDEN CAP

HOW TO GET THERE
Charmouth is off the main A35 road west of Morcombelake. Take the turning by the traffic lights, marked Beach and Car Parks, and follow it to the Pay and Display Beach car park.

LENGTH AND SEASON
$8^1/_2$ miles, some of it quite steep. Best April to October.

THE WALK
Cross the footbridge over the river. There are Wagtails, occasional Kingfishers, and Swans have nested. The beach, as well as its famous fossils, usually has Gulls, Oystercatchers, Cormorants, passing Terns, and perhaps surprises like Great Skua.

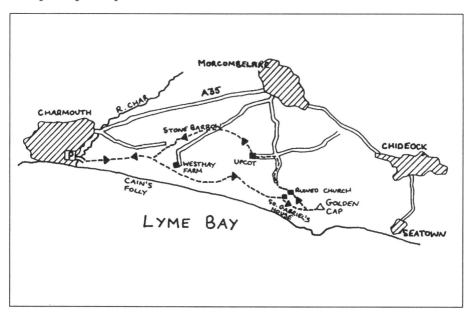

Climb up the hill, where the rare Small Blue butterfly can be seen. Marjoram, Wild Thyme and Parasol Mushrooms grow in the short grass, Cowslips on the edge of the neighbouring field, Primroses and Orchids where parts of the cliff have slipped – the undercliff. Kestrels hover overhead, Stonechats call from the Gorse, Wheatears pass by, and there is always a chance of a Peregrine, Fulmar or Raven. Charmouth is known for the declining Lesser Horseshoe Bat. Look for Grasshoppers and Bush Crickets, as well as the large black Bloody-Nosed Beetle, which ejects red fluid when threatened. There are Red Campion, Stitchwort, Warblers in the thickets, Skylarks overhead, Rabbits, Crows, and perhaps the smell of a Fox's earth.

At the top of Cain's Folly is a patch of heath with Heather, Gorse and Broom. Tormentil, Milkwort and Lousewort grow, Linnets, Meadow Pipits and Whitethroats nest, and Dartford Warblers have been known to visit. The undercliff has Roe Deer and Badgers. Take the steps down, listening for Yellowhammers and Green Woodpeckers. In marshy patches are Ragged Robin, Cuckoo Flowers, and sometimes Marsh Orchids. Cross a footbridge, then a second by an assortment of Ferns and Yellow Archangel. The path cuts a little inland, by a hedge on the left. Goldfinches hunt out Thistles and Teasels. After the third foot-bridge, the coastal path goes straight upwards. The slopes of Golden Cap are thick with Gorse as well as drifts of Bluebells in May. Cushions of Sea Campion, and a few Wild Strawberries, line the path. Butterflies include Small Copper, Dark Green Fritillary, Grayling and Small Heath. From the top of Golden Cap there is a magnificent view over Lyme Bay, with the chance of watching a soaring Buzzard from above.

Turn back from the top and retrace your steps. There is a chance of more Fritillary butterflies, Marbled Whites, Graylings and Green Hairstreaks. Slant inland past the ruined church, and by the thatched house turn right up the lane signposted Stonebarrow. Follow the lane with its ancient hedge of Hawthorn, Hazel, Blackthorn, and Sallow. Bryony, Honeysuckle, Travellers Joy and Vetch climb upwards, and Oak trees have Warblers and Tits. Turn left at the junction of lanes, still fol-

Golden Cap from the north-west

lowing the sign to Stonebarrow. The bridle path is lined with Umbellifers and scattered Foxgloves, Holly bushes attract Holly Blue butterflies. Swing right through Upcot Farm. A little beyond, on the left, is a fine Wild Apple tree.

The path emerges on an open hillside. Cross the stile by a signpost at the top right corner of the field, with Orchids. A little further on, on the right, is a gate marked with a yellow arrow. Go through and turn left, continuing left along the lane. There are Bluebells, Small Heath and Speckled Wood butterflies, Speckled Yellow moths, Warblers and Deer. At the signpost turn right, following the track marked Stonebarrow, then soon left over stile to find yourself back on the top of Cain's Folly. Walk straight to rejoin the coast path and so return down hill to Charmouth.

REFRESHMENT
There is a beach café by the car park. Charmouth has pubs and tea shops.

5. HARDY'S MONUMENT

HOW TO GET THERE

At Portesham turn off the B3157 to Winterbourne Abbas. After about two miles turn right, signposted Hardy Monument. There is extensive parking by the monument.

LENGTH AND SEASON

$7^1/_2$ miles. Best April to September.

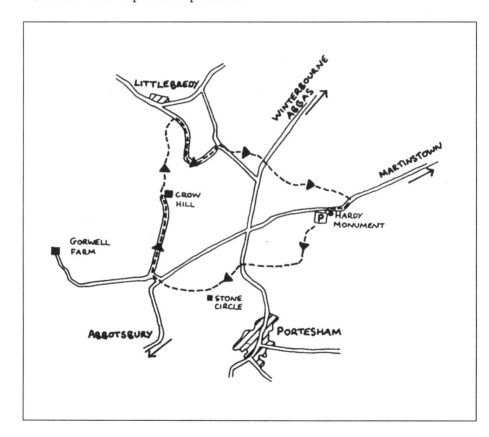

THE WALK

The land around the monument is dominated by Gorse and Heather. There are swathes of Bluebells in May, views in all directions, Whitethroats, Linnets, Stonechats, Grayling and Green Hairstreak butterflies, and the chance of Adders, especially on sunny days in March and April. At the far corner of the car park is a stone marking the inland route to West Bexington. Take the path downhill, watching for Sparrowhawks and Hobbies. The path drops into the mixed woodland with Speckled Woods, Jays, Foxgloves, Deer, Goldcrests and more Bluebells. Continue straight through the wood. After emerging, turn right by the signpost to West Bexington, then almost immediately left by a waymark and over a stone stile, continuing straight along the field edge with a stone wall on your left. The high fields are popular with Red Admirals, Painted Ladies, day-flying moths including the Silver Y, Buzzards and Skylarks. In winter there may be Lapwing and Golden Plover.

Join the road beside a barn, turn left, then almost immediately right by another signpost to West Bexington into a farmyard, with Stock Doves. Turn left by the waymark, then continue over a couple of stiles, following more waymarks to a track. There are many Yellowhammers, a small stone circle on the left (the stones thick with Lichens), Wall butterflies, Linnets, and strong-smelling Pineapple Weed underfoot. Beside crop fields listen for the 'wet-my-lips' call of the elusive Quail.

Follow the waymarks, skirting a small dell to the right, and continue along a scrubby hillside with blue Butterflies, Rabbits, Warblers, and some fine Woolly and Musk thistles. The gate on to the road, with a signpost beside it, is on the right. Turn right along the road, then left up a by-road, forking right along a track. The track is lined with Blackthorn which is thick with Sloes in autumn. Tree Pipits are occasional on the trees. Go left through a gate by the waymark, then skirt the copse that surrounds the farm buildings into another field. Continue by the edge of the copse until the path starts to go downhill, then strike out along a faint track over the huge rolling downland pasture, yellow with

Buttercups in summer. Look for Mushrooms in autumn. The track descends towards Little Bredy; there are views over the lake, and Mistle Thrushes in the trees. Pass the cricket pavilion (sometimes occupied by Rabbits!), then turn right on to the road. Red Kites visit the valley in winter.

The road is lined with fine Beech, Ash and Sycamore trees, with Tits and Jays. There are Buzzards overhead. The strip lynchets beside the road are rich in flowers, including Milkwort, Bird's Foot Trefoil and Cowslip. Butterflies include Small Copper,

Hardy's monument

Common and the fast-declining Adonis Blue. Field Forget-Me-Nots grow in the verge. At the road junction turn right, then after about quarter of a mile turn left along a track which skirts a small wood with Bluebells. Follow the waymarks to the right, with more Bluebell woods on the right. Roe Deer are common, and in early summer can be seen with their fawns. Cross the road and continue straight ahead with the Monument on the skyline, and the wood on the right.

Follow the track straight into the wood, then fork right uphill. There are Rhododendrons, Yellow Speckled Moths, Coal Tits, sometimes wintering Crossbills, and a chance of Nightjars on the woodland edges. Swing right at the next track, then right along the road, and so back to the Monument.

<u>REFRESHMENT</u>
The nearest pubs are at Portesham, Martinstown and Winterbourne Abbas.

6

KINGCOMBE MEADOWS

HOW TO GET THERE
From the Old Swan pub, Toller Porcorum, take the Kingcombe Road and continue straight to a sharp right turn. Just beyond, on the right is Pound Cottage, the reserve information centre, with a small car park.

LENGTH AND SEASON
$3^3/_4$ miles.

THE WALK
The tracks and paths at Kingcombe are sometimes fairly faint, and often muddy, so walkers should take care. Kingcombe is best visited between April and September.

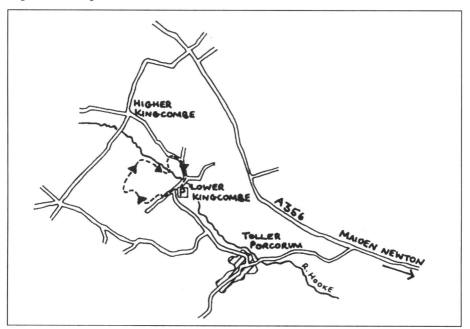

From Pound Cottage, where Grizzled Skippers have been seen, turn left along the road, then take the track straight in front. Garden and Willow Warblers sing in the undergrowth, with Blackcaps and Chiffchaffs higher up. The lane sides are thick with Primroses, Dog's Mercury, and Early Purple Orchids. Turn right through the gate into Coarse Mead, which has more Orchids, Lady's Mantle and the unusual Corky-Fruited Water Dropwort. Turn left and follow the hedge, where Warblers and Flycatchers nest and which includes a fine Crab-Apple tree, up to the pond, with Frogs, and occasional Toads and Grass Snakes. Great Spotted Woodpeckers have nested. Continue straight into the next field, a haze of Meadow Brown butterflies in high summer, then swing right by the lone Oak tree. The grass is starred with Violets in May, Bluebells grow in great swathes, Roe Deer visit. Cross a small trickle among hazels, with Wood Sorrel, and emerge on a small path that curves to the left. On the right is a Sphagnum bog with Cuckoo Flower, Cotton Grass, Lousewort, Bog Pimpernel, yet more Orchids, and Fritillary butterflies. Follow the track into the trees then turn left. There is a large sett where Badgers can be watched at dawn and dusk. Past the sett turn right across the next field to a stile in the left corner. Cross it, turn left and enter a large open field, with Buzzards overhead. Walk uphill, with a fine view, then cut down to the lone tree, and turn right along the path. There are more Violets and many species of butterfly, including Small Pearl Bordered Fritillary. Cross the line of trees into the next field and walk to the far left corner. Watch for Cuckoos, low Gorse, Heather, and some fine Thistles.

Follow the path through more trees into a smaller field, looking for Purple Hairstreaks, Nuthatches and Green Woodpeckers in the oak trees. Rabbits and Speckled Woods are frequent, the rare Marsh Fritillary occasional. The ground is boggy with Marsh Marigold and Iris. Ignore the gate on the left, turn right through hedges into a big bare field, and head across to the far left corner. There are Primroses, Bluebells and several species of Tit including the unusual Willow Tit. The path runs by the fence with the River Hooke just beyond. Look for brook Trout, Kingfishers, Grey Wagtails, and Dippers. Continue beside the river, watching for Goldcrests, together with Woodcock, Snipe, Redpoll and Siskin in the winter. Dragonflies and Damselflies are numerous, including the Emperor and Banded and Beautiful Demoiselles. There are interesting fungi in the autumn.

Where a fence blocks the way, turn right uphill. Cross a ditch into another field, then go through a gate on the left, and swing back left through trees to rejoin the river. Follow the river to the plank bridge, cross it and follow the waymark to a gap in the hedge. Blackcaps sing in the higher trees, and there is Ragged Robin. Cross the stile into Lords Mead, often a mass of meadow flowers in high summer, and turn right up to the gate, where there are Skippers. Hobbies sometimes pass overhead. Turn right along the road and follow it back to Pound Cottage.

REFRESHMENT

The Kingcombe Centre does teas on summer weekends. The Old Swan at Toller Porcorum (closed Tuesday lunch-time), does food.

7

LAMBERT'S CASTLE

HOW TO GET THERE
From Broadwindsor take the B3164 signposted to Lyme Regis and Axminster. At Birdsmoorgate turn left through Marshwood. Immediately after coming out of woodland turn very sharp left along a rough track and follow it to a car park.

LENGTH AND SEASON
6 miles. Best April to September.

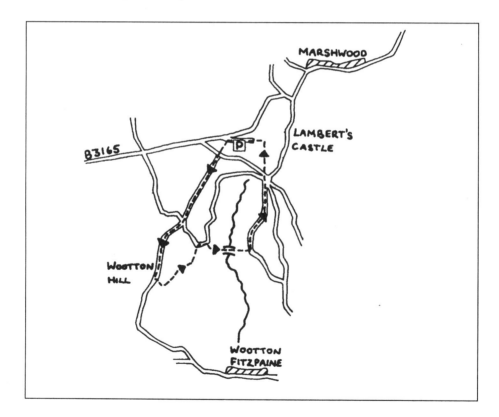

THE WALK

Return down the rough track, then turn left on to the open heathland. The heath has Broom, Stonechat, Adders, Linnets, Grayling and Marbled White butterflies, Meadow Pipits, occasional Whinchat. Walk straight, with the hedge on your left, cross the road and continue down a shaded bridleway with Sweet Chestnut trees, Jays, Speckled Woods, views over Marshwood Vale (where some years ago an escaped Golden Eagle hunted for some months), young Oaks with Oak Apples. There are a few Alder Buckthorns alive with bees in early summer. Badgers grub up the ground for earthworms. Further along the track is lined by an avenue of magnificent Beeches, some with huge, ancient Ivy plants on them.

Past some Rhododendrons join a road and continue straight, following the sign to Wootton Fitzpaine. The road plunges into the wood around Wootton Hill, with a mass of Beech trees; Holly may be worth checking for Holly Blues whilst there is a variety of Ferns, and masses of Violets in some of the banks. Chiffchaffs and Blackcaps call from the tree tops. There are Grey Squirrels and Tits everywhere, but the Roe Deer tend to be elusive because of the lack of undergrowth. There are patches where Bluebells and Ransoms grow thick in spring. Conifers nearby have Coal Tits and Goldcrests. Turn left off the road by the Forestry Commission car park, then continue straight on up the hill. There are Foxgloves, Silver-Washed Fritillaries, and patches of Wood Sorrel. Cross over the forest road and continue straight. Great Spotted Woodpeckers are common. Fungi in autumn are excellent and include Boletes. Where the path reaches the edge of the wood, go through the gate and continue straight along the grassy track.

Follow the track as it swings left, then go through the gate by a new house on to the road. Turn right and go downhill. There is Navelwort in the banks, Wild Rose and Honeysuckle in the hedge, Buzzards overhead. Turn right off the road by a waymarked gate, and continue straight downhill through the field, over a small stream by a bridge, then follow the track back up the hill, emerging through a farmyard on to a by-road. Turn left and continue uphill along the by-road. Red Admirals, Small Tortoiseshells and Peacocks visit the Brambles. There are unusual white Thistles, some patches of Bell Heather in the bank, and drifts of Hedge Bedstraw. Willow Warblers, Spotted Flycatchers and Whitethroats nest in the hedges. As the road climbs it shows a wide flowering verge which attracts butterflies, notably Large and Small Skippers.

At the main road continue straight, following the sign to Marshwood, then on up the footpath marked National Trust, Lambert's Castle Hill. Continue straight up the hill, with Grasshoppers and Crickets calling in summer, and so up on to the heathland at the top, with Purple Moor Grass, Birches, Rabbits and Small Heath butterflies. There are Mistle Thrushes, Great Spotted Woodpeckers, Bluebells, and some fine Scots Pines, which have had Crossbills. Just before the top of the hill, swing left and return to the car park. It is also worth checking the woodland edges of Lambert's Castle, which provide good opportunities of seeing Purple Hairstreak butterflies in the Oak tree tops in midsummer, and the outside chance of a summering Redstart, Wood Warbler, or even Pied Flycatcher.

REFRESHMENT
The Bottle Inn at Marshwood.

LANGTON HERRING

HOW TO GET THERE

From Weymouth take the B3157 towards Abbotsbury. The turning to Langton Herring is on the left, about 4 miles out of Weymouth. Follow the road to the edge of the village. Just past a left turn marked Fox Barrow House is a wide verge with room to park.

LENGTH AND SEASON

$8^1/_2$ miles. All year.

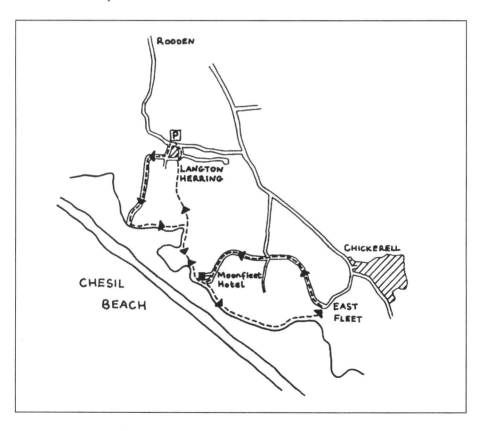

THE WALK

Follow the sign into the village, turn right before the church, then left by the bridleway sign. Follow the lane with fine views inland and over Lyme Bay. The lane is lined with Alexanders; Linnets and Whitethroats are common in the hedgerows, and there are some clumps of Wild Gladioli in the verge. The fields occasionally have Short-Eared Owl or even Hen Harrier in winter. At the cottages on the shoreline, turn left by the signpost to East Fleet/Weymouth, cross the stile, and continue along the field edge. Watch for Corn Buntings and Partridges on the field edges, both fairly unusual in Dorset. There are clumps of Great Hairy Willow-Herb, which sometimes attract Elephant Hawk-Moths. On the Fleet are Gulls, Herons, and Ducks, including, in winter, Merganser, Brent Geese, Wigeon, Teal, and a fairly good chance of more unusual species. Migrant butterflies like Painted Lady, Red Admiral, Peacock, and Small Tortoiseshell are frequent.

Cross a small stream and continue following the signposts to East Fleet. Wall butterflies favour the dry stone wall, which may also have Lizards. Gore Cove has Shelduck, Waders such as Dunlin, Grey Plover, Curlew, Godwit and Redshank, and Swans. Continuing beside the shore, past the Moonfleet Manor hotel, the steadily increasing salinity of the Fleet is shown by the changing shoreline vegetation and growing amounts of Sea Aster, Sea Arrowgrass, Shrubby Sea-Blite and Sea Lavender, as you walk south. There are also many Cockleshells, some of which have holes in them, caused by Oystercatchers. Mussels are rather less usual. Continue along the edge of a field, signposted to Weymouth, with the Fleet on your right, go through a spinney, with nesting Warblers, then swing back on to the shore. Little Terns from the colony at Ferrybridge sometimes fly over in the summer, as do Common Terns. In the migration season the Fleet often has unusual birds like Ospreys, Little Egrets, and Peregrines, and genuine rarities like American Wigeon turn up most years.

Where a small stream enters the Fleet, turn inland by the signpost to East Fleet and church, watching for Foxes. Pass the old smuggler's church, which has two fine Jacobean brasses, then turn left at the road and follow the shaded road under huge old Horse Chestnuts. Dogwood grows by the roadside. Green Woodpeckers, Jays, Warblers and Tits are all likely. Continue past the new church, and then where the road splits in three, take the middle way through the old gateway. The verge is thick with Cow Parsley and attracts Orange Tip butterflies in May and June. Small Heath, Meadow Brown and Gatekeeper butterflies are frequent in late summer. Blackcaps sing in the trees. Continue through Moonfleet Manor back to the shore, turn right, and retrace your steps along the coast path. Watch for Blue and Red Damselflies and Chaser Dragonflies. Rather than continuing by the coast over the stream, turn inland up a farm track to Langton Herring, turn right on to the road, left past the church, then right up the road to your car.

REFRESHMENT
The Elm Tree Inn at Langton Herring, and Moonfleet Manor Hotel for coffee and drinks.

9

MAPPERTON TO HOOKE WOODS

HOW TO GET THERE
From Beaminster take the B3163 towards Evershot and Maiden Newton.
A mile and a half out of the town turn right to Mapperton. Continue
straight past a left turn-off signposted Mapperton Gardens. 100 yards
on is a small car park on the right (small charge).

LENGTH AND SEASON
10 miles. Best April to November.

THE WALK
Turn right out of the car park and after 20 yards go through a gate on the
left. Cross the field, often alive with Pheasants and with Mapperton

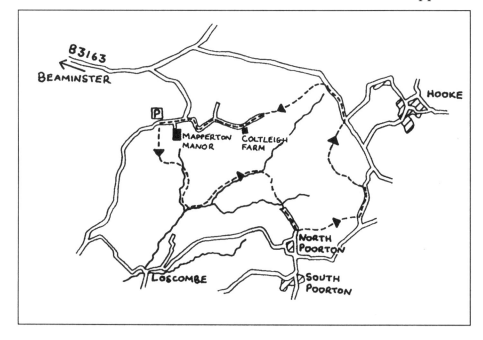

Manor on the left. Through the gate at the far end and turn right along a by-road. Go through another gate on the left along a downhill track. Buzzards hunt overhead. Watch for Little Owls. A small stream is rich in Watercress. Horse Mushrooms and other fungi grow in the grass. Hemp Agrimony attracts Peacock butterflies. Other butterflies include Marbled White, Skippers, Common Blue, Small Heath, and Orange Tip. Through a gate at the bottom you pass a mixed deciduous wood, worth checking for Woodpeckers and summer Redstarts, and including a fine Sweet Chestnut tree. Tits and Warblers are common, as are Roe and Fallow deer.

After 2 miles the track curves in towards a stream. Grey Wagtails visit, and Dipper is possible. (Over the stream is a track on the left to the DTNC reserve at Loscombe, with Orchids, Snakeshead Fritillaries). There are rumoured to be escaped Wild Boar in the area. Turn left and climb the hill by a stand of Oaks with Purple Hairstreaks in summer. Look for Jays, Grey Squirrels, Treecreeper and Nuthatch. In the grass are Parasol Mushrooms and Grass Snakes and Pheasants everywhere. I have seen a White Buzzard. The main track goes in and out of a small Hazel wood where there may be Dormice. At a waymarked gate, offering three tracks, take the right-hand one and ford the stream. Climb to an open field with strip lynchets, frequented by Skylarks and Pipits. Ahead is a steep hidden valley. Follow the track down to a muddy by-way, and turn right, then left around the cottage. Where the by-road swings right, take a blue-arrowed footpath left over a gate. There is a Hazel wood on the left, and a view right over North Poortown with its spired church. The Blackthorns are rich in Sloes and crawled over by trailing Bryony. Go through a waymarked gap in the hedge and on to a waymarked stile at the end of the next field.

Cross the field and follow the wood edge to the left. There are Field Mushrooms, Ink-Caps and Russulas. Badgers dig in the grass for Worms. Violets and Dog's Mercury grow under the trees. Where the wood swings out, enter it, then turn right and follow the waymarks through Hooke Wood, alive with fungi in autumn, including Stinkcaps,

Puffballs, Boletes, Lactarius species, and many others. Winter Crossbills are occasional in the conifers. Cross a stile on to the road and turn left. Snowdrops in early spring. Turn left along a large track back into the wood, then fork right. Pass John Makepeace's extraordinary houses. This is among the best Bluebell woods in Dorset. Return to the road and turn left. There are Wild Raspberries by the roadside, Sparrowhawks dash past. Beyond the wood go left through a waymarked gate. Yellowhammers on the slopes, Barn Owls hunt the field and Red Kite has visited in winter. Continue straight with the hedge on your right until you reach the road by Coltleigh Farm. Snipe lurk in wet depressions. Follow the road straight, with views south to the sea and ahead to Mapperton Manor. At the road junction continue straight, the car park is on the right.

REFRESHMENT
Pubs, restaurants and tea-shops in Beaminster.

10

PILSDON PEN AND RIVER SYNDERFORD

HOW TO GET THERE

Take the B3164 from Broadwindsor, signposted Axminster, Lyme. Just past the left turn to Pilsdon and Shave Cross there are parking spaces.

LENGTH AND SEASON

9¹/₂ miles. Best April to September.

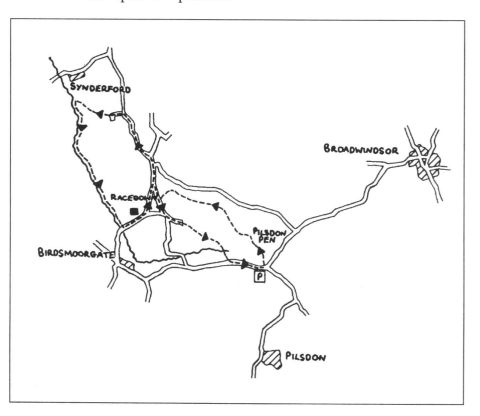

THE WALK

Cross the road and climb up the slopes of Pilsdon Pen, 908 feet high and the highest hill in Dorset, with magnificent views. There are Yellowhammers, Rabbits, Skylarks, Pipits, Gorse and Heather. Butterflies include Large Skipper, Wall and Grayling. Cross the old hill fort and at the far end turn left down to the bottom of the hill, go through the gate on the right and go diagonally up the hill to the right. Cross by the waymarked stile and turn left. There are Buzzards overhead and Painted Lady butterflies. Follow the edge of the field round to the far right corner and over another waymarked stile. There are Bluebells, including unusually many white ones, in the hedge. Walk beside the line of Oak, Ash, Hawthorn and Holly trees. Watch for the striking Brimstone moth on Hawthorn.

Follow the waymarks across the next field, over another stile and beside a line of Beech and Sycamore trees. Roe Deer and Foxes can be seen. Follow the edge of the field round to the left, the hedge having many Foxgloves. Cross the stile in the far left corner and follow the waymark to the right through the gate and straight across the next field. A felled Beech has some magnificent Bracket Fungi. Go through the next gate and turn right along the road. At Coles Cross turn left along the road to Winsham. The hedges have Finches and Tits. Pass the waymark on the left and turn left into Causeway Farm. Turn right just before the farm through a gate, then swing left over another gate by a yellow waymark, cross the next field, then follow the right-hand edges of the fields beside a small wood, where Buzzards and Tawny Owls often nest. The full-grown Beeches are worth scanning for Redstart, Wood Warbler or Pied Flycatcher.

On reaching the River Synderford do not cross it, but turn left and begin to follow it. For the next 2 miles keep beside the river, with it on your right, crossing gates and stiles where they appear. The Synderford is a pretty little stream with well-treed banks, Bugle and Cuckoo Flower, drifts of Ransoms and Bluebells; Woodpeckers, Warblers, Flycatchers, Long-Tailed Tits, Thrushes and Nuthatches; Squirrels, Mayfly hatches.

Dippers have visited. Damselflies include the Beautiful Demoiselle, Common Blue and Blue-Tailed. There are varieties of Mushrooms and fungi, and the commoner brown butterflies including Speckled Wood and Wall, as well as the Green-Veined White and Orange Tip. Eventually, past a line of poplar trees, there is a farm on the left and a small lake on the right with nesting Canada Geese and Pied Wagtails. The path becomes a lane, follow it, fork right, then turn left along the road, up the hill. There are Violets growing in the bank, and a Rookery near Racedown House, where Wordsworth stayed.

Follow the road round, then turn right where you came out on the road earlier, follow the track straight, then fork left. Butterflies include Painted Lady, Red Admiral, Small Tortoiseshell, Peacock and also the Silver Y moth. Follow the bridle path, cross the gate by the barn, and continue straight with the hedge on your right. The foot of the hedge is pierced by many burrows. Watch for hunting Stoats. After reaching the road turn left and return to your car.

REFRESHMENT
The Rose and Crown at Birdsmoorgate, the White Lion at Broadwindsor and the café restaurant at the Broadwindsor Arts Centre.

POWERSTOCK COMMON AND EGGARDON HILL

HOW TO GET THERE

From Maiden Newton follow the A356 to Crewkerne for a mile, turn left to Toller Porcorum (**not** Toller Fratrum). Turn right by the Old Swan pub, then after a mile left into Clift Lane. Take the first left, then left again, go under the old railway bridge. A small car park is just past the bridge on the right.

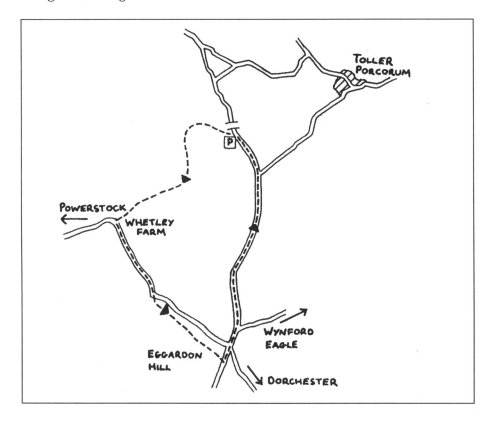

8 miles. Best April to October.

Follow the track to Powerstock Common. Throughout the reserve are good chances of seeing Woodpeckers, Deer, Foxes, Nuthatches and Treecreepers. Where the track divides take the right fork, then left along the edge of the open stretch of heath where Adders and Lizards bask in hot weather, especially among the piles of felled timber. The path leads into a wood and past two ponds. The larger is used by all three species of British Newt, and in March there are long strings of Toad spawn in the water. Powerstock Common in May and June is excellent for Orchids and rarer butterflies, especially Small Pearl Bordered and Silver Washed Fritillaries and Wood Whites, as well as Skippers and huge numbers of Ringlet, Meadow Brown and Gatekeeper.

The path curves round and crosses another path. Roe Deer often hide in the thickets. Edible Ink-Cap Mushrooms are common in autumn. Continue straight, past old once-laid Oak trees. There are Warblers and occasional Nightingales in summer. Dormice search out nuts in the Hazel thickets on late summer evenings, Weasels dart across the rides, and Deer are often seen. The path climbs up into a sea of Bracken. There is a Badger sett just to the right, and a fine view on the left. Woodcock and Tree Pipit sometimes appear on the woodland edge and Buzzards soar overhead. Escaped Wild Boar have been seen. Coming down the hill, take a turning left into a wet wood of Sallow and Stinking Iris. The path continues relatively straight, emerging into the fields where a track leads through Whetley Farm to the road. Turn left and follow the road up to Eggardon Hill.

Eggardon is the last outcrop of the chalk uplands of south-east England. An old hill fort (storage pits are visible on the right of the track by the main Bridport road), it offers superb views over Lyme Bay. Grazed by sheep and owned by the National Trust, Eggardon in late summer is rich in plants, notably Wild Thyme, Milkwort, the small purple Autumn Gentian, Bee Orchid, Rock Rose, and Eyebright. Swifts hunt overhead in high summer and autumn migrants include Wheatears, Chats, and flocks of Swallows and Martins sometimes accompanied by hunting Hobbies. Hoopoes have been seen. Skylarks and Pipits nest, as do occasional Red-Legged Partridges. In winter there is always the chance of a Raven, or even a Red Kite. Eggardon is a haven for smaller, less common butterflies like Grizzled and Dingy Skippers and Chalkhill and Adonis Blues.

From Eggardon take the left-hand road signposted Toller Porcorum. The fields on the left are often used by a large herd of Fallow Deer, which includes several white animals. Barn Owls occasionally hunt here in the winter dusk, and the verges in spring are rich with Primrose, Red Campion, Bluebell, Wood Anemone and Stitchwort. Ignore the right turn to Toller Porcorum and continue straight between banks that are covered with strong-smelling Ransoms in April. Tawny Owls call in the woods. Jays and Grey Squirrels are hard to miss, especially in autumn. Powerstock Common car park is on the left.

REFRESHMENT
The Old Swan at Toller Porcorum, The Three Horseshoes at Powerstock and The Spyway Inn at Askerswell.

12

WYNFORD EAGLE

HOW TO GET THERE

From the centre of Maiden Newton follow the A356 towards Crewkerne, take the first left over the river, then turn sharp right. At the village of Wynford Eagle, park on the left-hand verge by a barn, a few yards up the road signposted to West Compton.

LENGTH AND SEASON

7 miles. Best April to September.

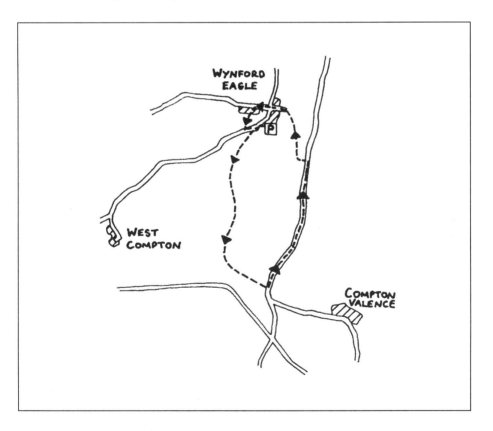

THE WALK

Walk down the West Compton road. Swallows nest in the farm. The fields have flocks of wintering Gulls and Lapwings. Where the road swings right, turn left by a waymark. There are superb views over the village and stream, and large numbers of Pheasants, Stock Doves, Linnets and Crows. Cuckoo Pints grow in the hedgerow as do Primrose and various species of Thistle, Campion, and Vetch. The hedgerow is an ancient one, combining Hazel, Elder, Hawthorn, Holly, Ivy, Wild Rose, Blackthorn, Ash and Field Maple. The field edges have Scentless Mayweed, Corn Marigold and Poppies.

Continue straight, Skylarks and Pipits are present all year. Fallow and Roe Deer frequent the hills. Foxes and Rabbits are common. In winter fields with stubble attract flocks of Finches and Buntings. Barn Owls occasionally hunt in the evening. One summer rare Montagu's Harriers nested in a nearby cornfield. Where a hedge blocks the track go through a small waymarked gate, then another gate, and cut across a small field to the far left corner, past an ancient earthwork. On the left is a quarry, where Crows and sometimes Kestrels nest in the ash trees. Through another waymarked gate the fields have Lapwing and Golden Plover in winter. There is a chance of a Hare, though generally they are shy. In May and June Rapeseed crops attract swarming Bees and Corn Buntings nest nearby. Quail and Hobby are possible in summer, Peregrines in winter. Go through the gate at the corner of the next field, turn right by the waymark and follow the edge of the field until reaching the road by a barn.

Turn left along the road and follow it for $1^1/_2$ miles. Fieldfare and Redwing visit in winter. In summer the stands of Cow Parsley and other Umbellifers are thick with Soldier Beetles. Butterflies include Brimstone, Orange Tip, Blues, Marbled White and Small Heath. Watch for Red-Legged Partridge and Grasshoppers. A small conifer plantation on the right has Coal Tits and Goldcrests. There are several species of Fern on the verge. Little Owls hunt.

By a large modern farm turn left off the road at the blue arrow way-mark, then right over the next gate. Goldfinches, Willow Warblers and Whitethroats are frequent in the scrub. Cuckoos call in spring, Stonechats are casual in winter. Buzzards nest in the wooded valley. Scabiouses and other chalk-loving plants grow in the turf. Follow the track past a quarry on the right, swinging left down into Wynford Eagle through a farmyard. Follow the Bridport road over the river where Grey Wagtails are often seen and occasionally Dippers (they are commoner downstream at Maiden Newton, as are Kingfishers). Turn left by the church, which has a fine old carving of two wyverns near the door. Cross the stile by the church wall and follow a small avenue of beech trees, worth checking for winter Bramblings. At the next field turn left and cross the river on a plank bridge. The river is lined with Watercress and attracts wintering Snipe and Green Sandpiper. In spring there is Cuckoo Flower and Marsh Marigold. Climb the hill to the road and turn left back into the village.

REFRESHMENT
There are two pubs in Maiden Newton and a fine bakery.

13

LODMOOR AND RADIPOLE LAKE

HOW TO GET THERE
Lodmoor is just north of Weymouth on the A353 to Preston. Take the first right after Lodmoor Country Park, there is a pay and display car park.

LENGTH AND SEASON
2¹/₂ miles. All year.

THE WALK
Cross the road and continue straight to the Tollhouse hide where there is a blackboard telling what is around. Stands of Michaelmas Daisies

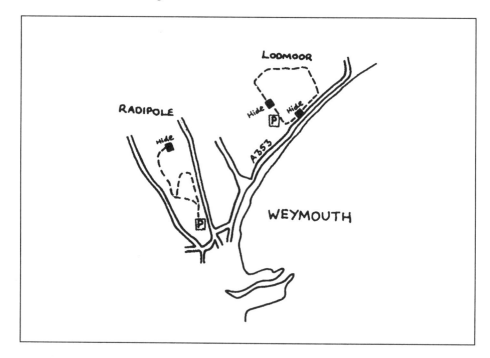

attract butterflies in autumn. Waders like Redshank, Snipe, Greenshank, Ruff, Sandpipers and Black-Tailed Godwits can include extreme rarities such as Sociable Plover (1995), Lesser Yellowlegs (1993). In winter there are large flocks of Lapwing, Teal and Wigeon with smaller numbers of Pintail, Shoveler and Golden Plover. Brent Geese are occasional. Little Egrets are becoming commoner. Terns visit, as do rarer Gulls such as Iceland, Little and Mediterranean. Beyond the Tollhouse hide is a sluice with Wagtails, then scrub with Wild Roses and Travellers' Joy which often contains migrating Warblers. The chances of a spring Garganey are better here than anywhere else in Dorset. Yellow Wagtails used to be common, but are now only occasional. Weymouth Bay, across the road, has Divers and Grebes in winter. Turn left. The reed beds on the right have Bearded Tits, Cetti's Warblers, Water Rail. Keep to the left, past the houses, watching out for Butterbur, butterfly-haunted Buddleia, and Periwinkle in the hedge. Some larger fungi can be seen in autumn. Southdown hide is on the left, Silverweed sprinkles the grass and there are views over the marsh where Foxes and Roe Deer are seen. Several sorts of Dragonfly breed and Lodmoor is known for a striking black and yellow striped Spider. Keep turning left through the reed bed, watching for Water Pipits. Melcombe hide is probably the best for birds. Teal can be exceptionally approachable. Return to the car park.

From Lodmoor drive back into Weymouth, turn right by the Coronation Clock, and turn right by the bridge. Park by Radipole Lake, either pay and display or get a ticket from the RSPB reserve centre.

Visit the centre with information on what is about. As with Lodmoor any sort of bird can turn up in spring and autumn. In winter Water Rail are easier to see here than anywhere else in England, and Spotted Crakes visit most autumns. Gulls often include rarities, and there are waders at passage times, especially Snipe, Duck and Herons. Cross the bridge and walk through the reed beds with Bearded Tits, Reed and Sedge Warblers and Reed Buntings. Harvest Mice are there but rarely seen. Turn first right and follow the waterside path with Grebes and sometimes very visible fish. Cetti's Warblers are noisy in the scrub. As the path swings to the left, there is a large lake on the right with diving Ducks and Scaup in winter, and huge gatherings of Swift, Swallow and Martins in autumn. There are butterflies on the Buddleia bushes. Continue to the next bridge, turn right and cross it, walking up to the north hide with Kingfisher, Herons, Emperor Dragonflies. The fields have Foxes and Cuckoos in spring. The path is lined with Reed Mace, Comfrey and Water Forget-Me-Not. Grasshopper Warblers call in spring. Rarer plants include Orchids and Summer Snowflake. There are Hawk, Burnet and Tiger Moths in summer. Butterflies include Holly Blue, Wall and Marbled White by the gate. Return to the bridge the same way, then take the straight path back to the visitors' centre and car park.

REFRESHMENT
Weymouth has cafés, restaurants, pubs and so forth in huge numbers.

14

PORTLAND BILL – WESTON

HOW TO GET THERE
From Weymouth cross Ferrybridge on the A354, then follow the signs through Fortuneswell and Easton to Portland Bill. Park at the car park there (charge).

LENGTH AND SEASON
6 miles. Best for birds in spring and especially autumn; flowers and butterflies in summer.

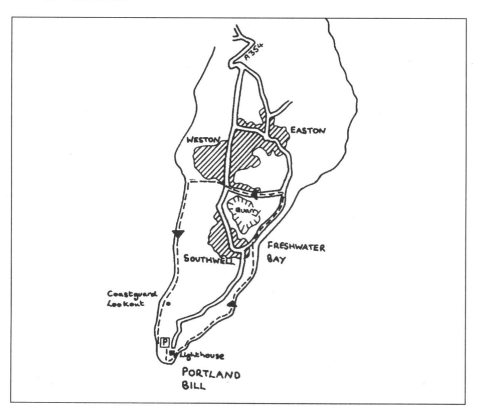

THE WALK

Walk down to the Bill and look out over the Race, where the water is choppy. There are often Gannets fishing, Shearwaters, Skuas and other seabirds pass by. Dolphins are seen fairly frequently, Pilot Whales rarely. Purple Sandpipers are on the rocks in winter. Walk left, up the east coast, watching over the unenclosed fields, and the sea. Cormorants dry their wings on rocks. Flowers include Rest Harrow, Lady's Bedstraw, Sea Lavender, and the delicate Pale Flax. Thrift is everywhere. The old quarries have caves, old machinery, sometimes Little Owls, or Black Redstarts. Excellent views along the south Dorset coast. Butterflies include Skippers, Marbled White, Browns. The rocks are dyed with lichens.

Portland is famous for its migrant birds, especially in the autumn, and it is never possible to say what will turn up where. Warblers, Flycatchers, Buntings, Pipits, of many different kinds, can be in any bush or on any ledge. Shrikes, Hoopoes, wrynecks and other rarities are annual at Portland.

Continue along the coast path, above the low cliffs. Red (and White) Valerian grows strongly, whilst one quarry has a stunted Fig tree demonstrating the mildness of the winters. The small purple-flowered Venus's Looking Glass can be found. Watch for Golden Samphire and Portland Spurge. Skylarks and Pipits sing. Portland has its own sub-species of the Silver-Studded Blue butterfly, and there are also Common, Small, Chalkhill and Holly Blues. Cliff Rabbits dart along the ledges, Foxes hunt them. The path swings left to join the road. Turn right along the road, with the great quarries on your left. The roadside has Buddleia, sometimes attracting Tortoiseshells, Red Admirals and Painted Ladies. Travellers' Joy crawls over the walls, huge flocks of Finches feed on the Thistles. Small Heath butterflies flutter amidst the grass. There are stands of Fennel.

Turn left by the signpost to Weston and continue along the road, Weston Street. There are Woodpigeons, although trees are rare on

Portland; Swifts hunt overhead, the roadside is thick with Field Mallow. The large Privet hedges have had Privet Hawk moth caterpillars. At the next road junction, cross the road and go down the footpath signposted Barleycrates Lane. A Sparrowhawk has been known to hunt it. Keep to the main lane, turning left. Alexanders line the lane, and there are lots of Meadow Brown and Marbled White Butterflies.

At the cliffs, turn left, heading south. Over the sea are Gulls, Terns, Gannets, Cormorants, Oystercatchers. On the cliff top are Heath and Lady's Bedstraw, Rest Harrow, Knapweed, Wild Thyme, Eyebright, and Pyramidal Orchids. Watch for the rare Bastard Toadflax and Broom-rape. The butterflies are still mainly Browns, Blues, Skippers and Marbled White, with a chance of Dark Green Fritillary. There are wainscot moths. Fulmars cruise along the cliff top. Where the path swings left away from the cliff edge, by the MOD buildings, it is just possible to see the Kittiwake colony on the cliffs and hear them calling. Guillemots are on the sea below. Follow the fence round and scramble through the old quarry, with Scarlet Pimpernel, Wheaters (sometimes nesting), passage Redstarts, and Rabbits, to the high Pulpit Rock jutting out to sea. From here it is possible in spring to see Guillemots, Razorbills, and even occasionally Puffins, flying or on the water. They nest on the cliff just out of sight. The car park is immediately behind you.

REFRESHMENT
The Pulpit Inn near Portland Bill. There are also cafés near the car park.

15

MORETON

HOW TO GET THERE

From Dorchester take the A352 as far as the large roundabout beyond Broadmayne. Turn left on to the B3390, and follow it about three miles. Take the first right after the level crossing and continue straight into Moreton. On the left is a signpost 'To The Church'. Follow this and park beyond the post office.

LENGTH AND SEASON

7¹/₂ miles. Best spring and summer.

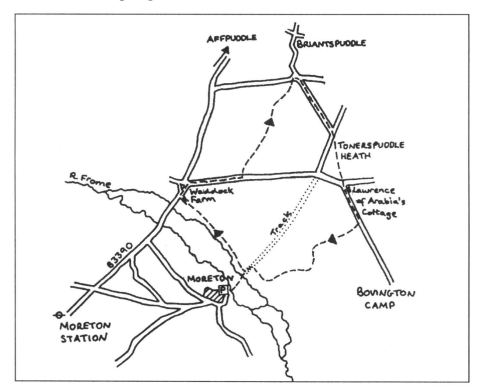

THE WALK

Cross the River Frome on the footbridge. Several species of fish can be watched in the clear water, Kingfishers and Grey Wagtails are frequent, Swans often nest. Banded Demoiselle Damselflies visit. Continue up the lane, watching for Silver-Washed Fritillaries. Beyond another small stream, turn left by a waymarked stile and continue along the path over farmland. On the left are views over the flood meadows, which in winter contain Duck and Snipe, and occasionally Bewick's Swans. Holly trees in the hedge may attract Holly Blues. The path is lined with cornfield weeds, including a fine display of Corn Marigolds, Chamomile, and Mallow. Stock Doves fly overhead and Kestrels. Butterflies include Skippers and Gatekeepers. Continue straight through Waddock Farm and along the by-road to the main road.

In the Frome Valley

At the road turn right, then right again signposted Wareham. Continue along the road into Oakers Wood, with fine deciduous trees, old Hazel coppices, fungi, Bluebells, Wood Sorrel. Tits, Nuthatches, Treecreepers are all present. Turn left off the road at the bridleway marked Culpeppers Dish. Rhododendrons line the path, there are Russulas and Fly Agaric in autumn, some unusual trees, Bluebells, ferns, White Admiral butterflies, and possibly Purple Hairstreaks high in the Oaks. Blackcaps and Chiffchaff sing. Rose of Sharon has escaped from a garden. Sparrowhawks hunt.

Follow the path straight, emerging onto a heath, with Ling, Bell and Cross-Leaved Heather, Pines, Tormentil. Green Woodpeckers hunt for Ants's nests. Stonechat, Linnet and Yellowhammer call. Rimsmoor Pond is on the right, with Dragonflies, occasional hunting Hobbies, Cotton Grass, white Water Lilies. Continue along the main track, ignoring the waymarked footpath to the left. A huge deep bowl on the left is Culpepper's Dish. Turn left at the road, then left again along the road marked Bovington. There are Jays and Long Tailed Tits in the trees, Rabbits, and fine views. The verges are rich in Hemp Agrimony, Vetch, Agrimony, St John's Wort, and Birds Foot Trefoil.

At the road junction cross straight over and follow a blue waymarked sandy path beside Turners Puddle Heath, with several sorts of Thistle, Ox-Eye Daisy, Centaury. Bear right along the military road, then turn right by the blue waymark and go through the fence on to the heath. There are Nightjars in summer, Dartford warblers, Silver-Studded Blue butterflies, Dorset Heath, Emperor Moth, possibly Twayblades. Go through the gate, and straight over the road to the road opposite marked Bovington Camp, passing Lawrence of Arabia's cottage, Cloud's Hill. Continue as far as the tank viewing area on the left, and turn right over a stile along a yellow-marked footpath beside a tank track. Continue downhill into the conifer woods with Goldcrest, Bullfinch, Coal tit, and Crossbills. Turn left at the next junction, then just past the next gate turn right and walk past an open area with young Pines, Birches, Honeysuckle. Turn right again, watching for Woodpeckers and Deer, clumps of Common Cow-Wheat. Left at the next junction, returning on to the path down to the footbridge over the river, with a fine old Yew on the left. Cross the river to your car.

REFRESHMENT
The Frampton Arms by Moreton Station. Also visit Moreton Church, with magnificent engraved windows by Laurence Whistler.

16

WORTH MATRAVERS

HOW TO GET THERE

From Corfe Castle take the B3069 through Kingston, then turn right to
Worth Matravers. The car park is just before the village on the right.
There is a small charge.

LENGTH AND SEASON

9 miles, some of it quite steep. All year.

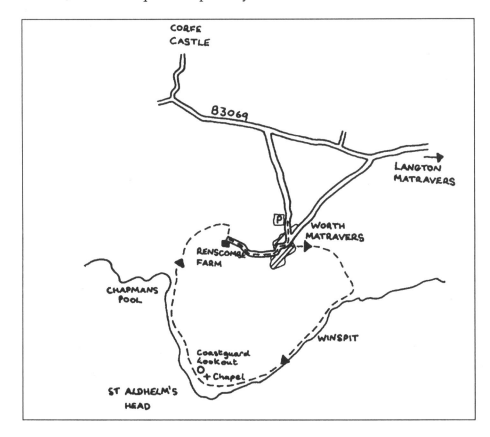

THE WALK

Set out to the right, past the pub, then right again. There are often Goldfinches in the village. Turn left by the little pond, left again marked to Seacombe, then left along a tiny path waymarked Seacombe. Cross a stile and go down the hill then up the opposite side. The field has Musk Thistles. Follow the path, swinging right down to the coast where Seacombe is signposted. There are Rabbits, Corn Buntings, Skylarks and Pipits in the fields. The rare Hoopoe has been seen. At the coast turn right and follow the Dorset coast path to the quarries at Winspit.

The Winspit valley, thick with Blackthorn, Traveller's Joy, Hawthorn and Ivy, is famous for bird migrants, including Warblers, Nightingale, Firecrest, Flycatchers, and most famously a Red-Flanked Bluetail in November 1993. Swallows linger to the end of October. The quarries at Seacombe and Winspit are well-known for Bats, including the Greater Horseshoe, Bechstein's and Grey Long-Eared. There are good chances of Black Redstart, Little Owl, and Ring Ouzel in spring and autumn. In the winter of 1969-70 a Wallcreeper wintered. Continue along the coast path. Wild Cabbage, Teasel, and early Spider Orchids grow near the cliff-edge. Rock Samphire, the unrelated Golden Samphire, and early Scurvy-Grass are in rock crevices. The parasitic Broomrape, with scales rather than true leaves, is worth looking for in high summer. The shy grey Bush-Cricket may lurk in coarse cliff-top grass. Offshore in spring and summer there are Shags, Fulmar, Kittiwake and Guillemots. There is a chance of Puffin or Razorbill, and passage birds include Shearwaters, Skuas, Seaduck, Gannets and Terns. Feral Pigeons nest in the cliffs as their Rock Dove forebears used to. In winter there are large flocks of Linnets and other Finches.

Around St Aldhelm's Head, where there is a coastguard watchpoint and St Aldhelm's Chapel, there is a good chance of Ravens and Peregrines. Rarer raptors pass by in autumn and winter. Stonechat are frequent. Vipers Bugloss grows here together with several unusual weeds such as Corn Gromwell. The fields are full of Partridges and stripe-winged Grasshoppers. The cliffs reach a height of about 450 feet.

There is a steep descent to the beach, and of course another equally steep rise back to the cliff top.

Butterflies are abundant and include Skippers, notably Lulworth Skipper, Green Hairstreak, Clouded Yellow, Small and Adonis Blues, Brown Argus and Marbled White. There is a chance of Dark Green Fritillary in high summer. Chapman's Pool sometimes has waders, usually Oystercatcher, and storm-driven Phalaropes turn up regularly in winter. Marshy patches have the Long-Winged Conehead Cricket. Kestrels are numerous on the downs, and there are Field Mushrooms. Follow the path as it swings inland, then turn right following the signpost to Renscombe. Cross the field, then turn left along the by-road, then right at the farm and follow the road back to Worth Matravers, with Alexanders thick in the verge. Keep straight past the church and pond, then turn left at the pub back to the car park.

REFRESHMENT
The Square and Compass Inn.

17

ARNE

HOW TO GET THERE

From Wareham take the A351 towards Corfe Castle. At Stoborough, just past the petrol station, is a tiny left turning marked Nutcrack Lane. Follow this straight about 3 miles to the RSPB car park on the right.

LENGTH AND SEASON

5 miles. All year.

THE WALK

From the car park walk up into the village; there are often Squirrels, Nuthatches and Treecreepers in the trees. Turn right, waymarked Shipstal Point, through a sheep farm. The fields have Fieldfare and Redwing in winter, Mushrooms in autumn, and Green Woodpeckers all year. Entering the reserve, turn right into the wood. There are several

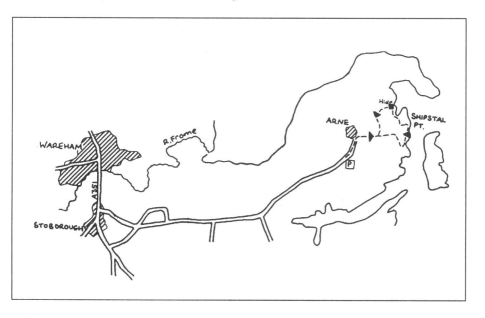

Sweet Chestnuts in among the Oaks, worth checking for Purple Hair-streak butterflies in summer, Birches and Holly trees. Roe Deer sometimes hide in the Bracken. Continue round the path, past the Rhododendron bushes. In autumn there are several forms of fungus.

You emerge on to a path of duck-boards. There are often Sika Deer to the right, Redshanks and Curlew visit the saltings, mainly made up of Cord Grass. The island opposite often has large wader flocks, especially Oystercatchers. Mergansers are frequent in the channel from October to May, Cormorants and Shelduck all year, and in winter there may be rarer Grebes and Seaduck. Summer sees frequent Sandwich and Common Terns among the Gulls. In the sand it is worth looking for Sea Campion. At the end of the beach turn left and walk up the track, then turn left again, up Shipstal Hill.

Arne is famous for its heathlands, though much of them are rarely open for visiting. This area of mixed Ling and Bell Heather generally has one or two nesting Dartford Warblers, Stonechats, and several species of butterfly, most notably Silver-Studded Blues and Graylings. Adders are most visible in March and April, Cuckoos in May and June. The reserve has several national rarities, notably the Heath Grasshopper, Sand Lizard and Smooth Snake, but all are hard to see. Dwarf Gorse grows in the Heather, and Dodder – a parasite of Heather. Climb to the top of the hill, then down the steps on the far side and back across the heath, going straight across one path into the woods. In summer evenings Glow-Worms can sometimes be seen. Arne is famous for its moths, including Hawk and Tiger moths. There are several ponds where Dragonflies breed, including the striking Emperor, the Broad-Bodied Libellula, Southern Aeshna and the rare Downy Emerald. Damselflies are also good. At dusk the pools are patrolled by Bats, and Nightjars can occasionally be seen, or more often heard.

The Pine wood is good for Tits, Woodpeckers and occasional Crossbills. Follow the path straight to the hide, from where there is a fine view over Poole Harbour. Little Egrets are probably commoner here than anywhere else in England, and Spoonbills are also frequent. There are huge numbers of waders, notably Spotted Redshank, Curlew, passage Whimbrel, Grey Plover, Dunlin and Black-Tailed Godwit, together with Teal, Wigeon, other Duck, occasional Kingfishers, wintering Harriers, a very visible herd of Sika Deer and occasional hunting Foxes. From the hide take the right-hand fork through the wood, notice how much better it has regenerated inside the deer fence, and then turn right and retrace your steps to the car park. In winter feeding stations encourage a variety of Tits, Finches and other small birds to come very close to the cars.

REFRESHMENT
There are several riverside pubs in Wareham, and the King's Arms in Stoborough.

18

STUDLAND

HOW TO GET THERE

Take the A351 to Corfe Castle, and just before the village turn left along the B3351 to Studland. Take the road through Studland towards the Sandbanks Ferry, then turn right signposted Knoll Car Park, National Trust. Charge for non-members.

LENGTH AND SEASON

7 miles. Any time of year.

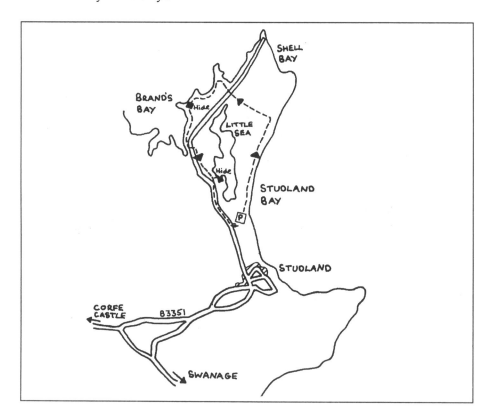

THE WALK

Walk through the Dunes car park to the far end, and follow the Heather Walk sign. There is Sheepsbit Scabious, Catsear, and Centaury in the grass. Turn left (not 'To The Beach') and follow the wide sandy track through the dunes, where Marram grass holds the sand in place. Watch for Grasshoppers. Warblers visit the scrub. Skippers and Brown butterflies, are common. All along this walk there is wealth of Dragonflies and Damselflies, including the Emperor, Broad-Bodied Libellula, Black and Ruddy Darters, Hawkers; and Emerald, Blue and Red Damselflies.

Continue along the main sandy track, swinging right, then left by the Studland Heath NNR sign. There are Linnets, Cross-Leaved Heath in damper places, Dodder in the Heather, and Sand Digger Wasps. Continue straight, following the Heather Walk arrow. Haresfoot Clover grows in low swathes. Heather is dominated by ling. Watch for Adders, especially in March-April, and there is a small chance of Smooth Snakes and Lizards. After about a mile, turn left by the yellow waymarked arrow. The path goes into the damp areas, dominated by Sallow and Birch, at the north end of the Little Sea, with Grass Snakes, Toads, Sedge

Studland cliffs

61

Warblers, a variety of ferns and fungi, and more Dragonflies and Damselflies.

The path emerges onto a mixture of Gorse and Heather, where Dartford Warblers can be seen. Wood Ants are busy, and their piled high nests can be seen. Cross straight over the road and continue along the path opposite. There are fine views over Poole Harbour, Brownsea Island and Castle. Common and Sandwich Terns fly past with several species of Gull. Stonechats call from the Gorse. There are Pipits and more chances of the elusive Dartford Warbler.

Cut straight across to the shoreline, then turn left and follow it. Oystercatchers, Redshank, Black-Tailed Godwits, Dunlin, Lapwing and other waders are usually present. Egrets are occasional. Herons, Cormorant, Shelduck are present all year; Grebes (especially Black-Necked), Divers, Brent Geese and Eider Duck visit in the winter. The Great Grey Shrike has also been seen in winter. The shore, with areas of salt marsh, is cloaked in Sea-Lavender, Samphire, Thrift, Sea Heath, Sea Campion, Sea Bindweed, Silverweed. Shoals of fry dart to and fro in the shallow water. There are some attractive outcrops of red sandstone as you continue along the shore, and a hide on the left overlooks Brands Bay towards the oil derrick.

Approaching the end of the inlet, by a broadish stretch of salt marsh, turn left between two Holly trees up a small path, and follow it to the road. There are Nightjars on the woodland edges. Cross the road to a path by the post and follow it a few yards, then turn left along a track parallel to the road. Watch for Grayling and Silver-Studded Blue butterflies, Stonechats, Dartford Warblers, Emperor Moths. After a few hundred yards there is a short right turn to the road. On the left the path curves away to the Little Sea, with a fine patch of Sundew on the right amidst some Cross-Leaved Heath, just under a Birch, before the lake. The lake has Bogbean, Yellow Iris, Water Mint, Bladderwort, and rarities like Yellow Bog Asphodel, and Marsh Gentian.

Turn left along the road. There are tall Holly bushes, and in the verge Ladys Bedstraw, Eyebright, Vetches, Squinancywort, unusual beetles, and Burnet Moths on the Knapweed. On the left is a stile, with a path leading through the wood to a hide with a beautiful view over the Little Sea, with Ducks and Grebes and occasional rarities. The wood has Roe Deer, Fox, Squirrels, Grass Snakes, Primroses, Bluebells, Tits, Jays, Fritillaries, White Admirals. Retrace your steps to the road, turn left and continue until you reach the left turn to Knoll Car Park; take it back to the car. Between August and April it is worth checking Studland Bay, just beyond the car park, for Divers, Grebes, Sea duck, Terns, and Auks.

REFRESHMENT
Café at National Trust shop by car park. Bankes Arms and tea shop in Studland.

NOTES